My Life As
An Astronaut

A Reflection of the Best. *Alan Bean's painting is a tribute to the thousands of Americans who made his trip to the Moon possible.* © *1987 Alan Bean.*

Just For Boys® Presents

My Life As An Astronaut

BY ALAN BEAN

as told to
Beverly Fraknoi

A Byron Preiss Book

A MINSTREL® BOOK

PUBLISHED BY POCKET BOOKS

New York   London   Toronto   Sydney   Tokyo

This book is a presentation of **Just For Boys®**, Weekly Reader Books.
Weekly Reader Books offers book clubs for children from preschool through
high school. For further information write to: **Weekly Reader Books,**
4343 Equity Drive, Columbus, Ohio 43228.

Published by arrangement with Pocket Books, a division of Simon &
Schuster Inc. Just For Boys and Weekly Reader are federally registered
trademarks of Field Publications.

Special thanks to Pat MacDonald, Robin Stevenson,
and Gwendolyn Smith.

Book design by Alex Jay/Studio J
Mechanicals by Mary LeCleir
Typesetting by David E. Seham Associates Inc.

Editor: Ruth Ashby

A MINSTREL PAPERBACK *ORIGINAL*

ISBN: 0-671-63452-6

First Minstrel Books Printing July 1988

A MINSTREL BOOK and colophon are registered
trademarks of Simon & Schuster Inc.

"My Life" is a trademark of Byron Preiss Visual Publications, Inc.

Printed in U.S.A.

CHAPTER ONE

Down.

From ten miles above the surface of the Moon, pitted and pocked with craters, we were heading down at last.

"Forty-five thousand feet," I called to Pete Conrad, commander of our mission. He stood barely two feet to my left at the controls of *Intrepid,* the rocket-powered Lunar Module that would actually take us to the Moon's surface. Far above, Dick Gordon was keeping watch from *Yankee Clipper,* the Command Module. While Pete and I were exploring, *Yankee Clipper* would orbit the Moon and wait for us to return.

"Nineteen thousand feet." For the moment, we were hurtling toward the Moon at nearly one hundred feet per second—more than a mile a minute.

"Looking good!" I called. A few seconds later a voice crackled over the radio, speaking to us over 239,000 miles of black and empty space.

"Intrepid, Houston. Go for landing."

At last we were nearly there. We'd come a long, long way and in a matter of minutes, we would come to rest on the rocky, dusty surface of the Moon. And I knew that, in all of history, only two human beings— astronauts Neil Armstrong and Buzz Aldrin—had walked on the Moon. Soon, Pete would become the third person to walk on this barren landscape. Then it would be my turn. It was a moment I had dreamed of, an achievement for which I had spent years working and training.

But, while *Intrepid* descended, there was no time to think about special moments. I had to keep my mind on my job, which was to keep track of our altitude and help direct the Lunar Module to a safe landing.

"Five hundred thirty feet, Pete. Four seventy-one. All right. Four twenty-six . . . four hundred . . . you're at three sixty-six." As I spoke, Pete was working the controls, slowing the *Intrepid*'s speed. Now we had slowed our descent toward the Moon's surface to barely five feet per second, then at three feet per second, then two.

"We're almost there," I announced. A moment later a tiny blue light flashed on the console in front of Pete. It meant that *Intrepid*'s landing legs were five feet above the lunar soil.

"Contact light!" Pete called over the radio to the engineers and scientists watching and waiting at Ken-

The crew of Apollo 12, Pete, Dick and me, in front of the Lunar Module Intrepid. *[NASA]*

nedy Space Center in Florida, back on Earth. Less than five seconds later, I felt a firm thump and Pete pressed the engine-off button. We had officially landed on the Moon.

That was all in November, the year 1969, a few days before Thanksgiving would be celebrated back on planet Earth. If you have read books on space, maybe you've seen pictures of *Intrepid*. Or maybe you remember watching on television as a sleek rocket blasted off toward space, pushed by the beautiful, fiery thrust of its powerful engines.

I know *I* remember such things. Becoming an astronaut was one of the most exciting, most satisfying things that has ever happened in my life. Today, more young people than ever are preparing themselves for careers in space. I can say only, how lucky they are! I'm lucky, too, because I not only *went* to space and have wonderful memories of my adventures; now, I am also able to spend time with brushes and paint, recording my memories for the world to see. It's like having those exciting times all over again. But I'll tell you more about my space paintings later.

What exactly is an astronaut? What kind of person do you have to be to travel into space? You probably think you already know the answer to the first question. An astronaut is someone who flies on a rocket into space, right? Well, yes, naturally—an astronaut *does* do that. In fact, the word *astronaut*, which comes

4

The Apollo 12 insignia and official crew patch for the United States' second lunar landing mission. The boat shown here is a clipper ship, after which the Command Module, Yankee Clipper, *was named.* [NASA]

from the Greek language, means "sailor to the stars."

People have dreamed of sailing among the stars for a very long time. According to one legend, an ancient king of Persia was one of the first people to travel into space. As the story goes, he was carried away from Earth on a chariot pulled by four magical eagles. That's only a folktale, but what a lovely idea it must have seemed to the young people who listened to it on warm summer evenings as they looked up at the starry night sky!

In real life there's much more to being a star sailor than simply stepping into a magic chariot—or even climbing into a spacecraft atop a modern rocket and flying off to orbit the Earth or walk on the Moon. Just like a car mechanic or a school teacher or a business executive, an astronaut on a space mission always has a serious job to do. On my Moon flight, I was assigned to be the pilot of the Lunar Module. Along with Pete Conrad, I was supposed to set up scientific experiments on the Moon itself, make scientific observations, and gather samples of Moon soil and rocks for scientists back on Earth to study. On my second trip into space, I had the responsibility of commanding the flight, and there was even more scientific work to do. That was the Skylab III mission. We lived for fifty-nine days, some 270 miles above the Earth, in America's first space station. We studied the Sun, the stars, the Earth, and the physical reactions of human beings to space.

Astronauts have always had to be willing to work hard. And they've always had to be courageous. The first human being ever to rocket into orbit around the Earth—only a quarter century ago—was a brave pilot from the Soviet Union. His name was Yuri Gargarin, and his spacecraft, called *Vostok,* streaked into the sky on a sunny, peaceful April morning. At the time, no one knew—not *really*—what would happen to the human body outside Earth's gravity; would a human be able to live in weightlessness? And no one knew whether the *Vostok* spacecraft would work properly and whether Gargarin, or any space explorer, would be able to return safely to Earth. But an hour and forty-eight minutes later when Gargarin came floating down under a parachute into a farmer's field, the world had its answer. From then on, in spite of the risks, humankind was aiming for the stars!

Like Yuri Gargarin, most early astronauts (and cosmonauts, as they are called in the Soviet Union) were chosen because they were top-notch aircraft test pilots. Test pilots lived with danger—and the un-known—every day. America's first astronaut group, the seven Mercury astronauts, were all seasoned test pilots. And they were all members of a military ser-vice, such as the Air Force, the Navy, or the Marine Corps. All were highly disciplined and in superb phys-ical condition. Today the situation is a bit different: A modern space traveler may be a physicist, a biologist, an engineer, a mathematician, or have some other special training. Even so, courage, dedication, and physical fitness are still part of the basic "gear" needed to become a sailor to the stars.

People are not the only creatures who have traveled into space. Spiders, bees, mice, frogs, green plants—even chimpanzees and dogs—have flown into orbit. Many have been part of scientific tests that have helped us learn about how living things can adapt to conditions in space.

Mercury astronaut Alan B. Shepard, Jr. became the first American to journey into space. His spacecraft, which he named the *Freedom 7,* flew for fifteen minutes. It climbed 116 miles above the Earth. Like any astronaut, Shepard had been rigorously trained for his adventure. Then, as now, the scientists and planners at NASA—the National Aeronautics and Space Administration—knew that it would be foolish to send a person into the foreign realm of space without his having as much knowledge and preparation as possible.

For the Mercury, Gemini, and Apollo astronauts, training meant hours of tiring physical tests and months of drills on tasks they would have to do while in space. It was pushing levers and tripping switches over and over again—and then once more for good measure. It also meant being spun around at dizzying speeds in an enormous centrifuge. If you've ever whirled around in a fast-moving ride at the amusement park, you know that when the ride goes fast, your body feels as if something heavy is pressing on it. When a rocket first lifts off from Earth, the astronaut hears a lot of noise and feels a lot of vibration. As the fuel is used up during the launch, the rocket accelerates, and he feels an increasing pressure pushing him back in his seat. The rides in the centrifuge were to prepare the astronauts for the forces they would actually experience when they finally rocketed into space.

There were many long months of studying. Even though I was an experienced test pilot before I joined the corps of astronauts, and already knew a good deal

The Hammer and The Feather. *By dropping a hammer and a feather at the same time, Apollo 15 astronaut Dave Scott again confirmed Galileo's finding that gravity pulls all bodies equally regardless of their weight. Painting © 1986 Alan Bean.*

9

about flying, I still had to learn all the complicated do's and don'ts of operating a spacecraft. That knowledge was important: One day my life and those of my fellow astronauts—or at least the success of our mission—might depend on it. I also had to learn how to properly carry out scientific experiments and to take photographs that would help scientists on Earth understand what lies beyond our planet. Studying science—that is, learning more about the world and the universe we live in—is a vital part of being an astronaut. Because it is so important, many of the people being chosen to become astronauts today are trained scientists. They are called mission specialists, and for them the biggest challenge is learning how to do their jobs in space.

You know that an astronaut is someone who works hard, is courageous, and tries to have the knowledge and skills to get the job done. But I think there is more to being a space traveler. Like Christopher Columbus or Marco Polo, the men and women who go into space are explorers. Exploring is part of being human; people have always wanted to know what lies beyond the next mountain or across a faraway river. Partly, it is just our natural curiosity: What is a place like? What would it be like to live there? Before the first Moon landing, I suppose there were even people who wondered if the astronauts would find lumps of green cheese! We didn't, of course. Instead, we performed experiments and brought back moon rocks that told us many new facts about the Moon itself and our planet Earth.

Astronauts are also trying out life in a new and different place. And what a life it is! For example, have you ever wondered what it would be like to float, light as a feather, because your body is suddenly weightless? Or to watch your morning orange juice curl up in a perfect ball and hang in front of you in midair? Think of trying to eat when your food keeps floating off your plate! Or imagine doing what I did—eating spaghetti on the Moon!

For a space explorer, there is always something new just around the corner. Maybe it is only learning how to eat in zero gravity, or maybe it is something more important, such as making a scientific discovery. Or maybe it is looking out the window of a lunar module and seeing a place—a dusty crater on the Moon— where no human being has ever set foot before.

Over the years, space travelers have turned many new corners. There have been failures and disappointments—and even a few terrible tragedies, such as the loss of the space shuttle, *Challenger*. Fortunately, though, there have been many more wonderful triumphs. Not long after Alan Shepard's historic flight, John Glenn became the first American to actually fly in orbit around our planet. Since those pioneering days, men and women from many countries have

November 19, 1969. I took this picture of Pete Conrad unfurling the American flag on the lunar surface. It was a proud moment for both of us. [NASA]

traveled to space. Twelve Americans have visited the Moon. Astronauts have docked space vehicles while floating in orbit—something that is very difficult to do. They have learned how to "walk" in space, and to repair satellites that enable us to forecast Earth's weather or to pick up the telephone and call someone thousands of miles away in Europe, Africa, or Asia. People have lived and worked in orbiting space laboratories, where they've conducted scientific experiments that would be impossible on Earth. As a bonus, sailors to the stars have experienced the thrill of looking back from the dark of space and seeing the beautiful blue ball studded with fluffy white clouds, which is our home, the Earth.

I have been fortunate enough to do most of these things. If you are reading this book and perhaps dreaming of becoming an astronaut, one day you might do them, too, and many more besides. But every dream has to start somewhere. I didn't just wake up one morning and find myself in a spacecraft on my way to the Moon. No, the road to my dream started long before I was officially accepted into the corps of astronauts.

Where did the road begin? As it happens, my life started far from the high technology and great achievements of the Space Age. It began in a most unlikely spot—a dusty corner of western Texas—in a sleepy little town called Wheeler.

CHAPTER TWO

I was born in Wheeler, Texas, on March 15, 1932. I don't remember much about Wheeler, because our family moved to the state of Louisiana before I was one year old. But I know that Wheeler was a tiny place, and I know that it was near a river. My father, Arnold Bean, was an expert on flood control. Most of his life he worked for the United States government. His job was to find the best place to build dams on a river and to help people on farms and in towns protect their property from the damage caused by floods. So wherever he took our family to live—and he took us many places—there was always a river nearby.

The first thing I really remember is being a very little boy in Minden, Louisiana. Minden was bigger than Wheeler, with lots of stores. I would tag along with my mother—who had the beautiful Irish name of Frances Caroline Murphy Bean—to go looking in all the windows. For Mom the move to a real town, even a not-very-big one, must have been exciting. She was the kind of person who was always looking for something to do.

Of course, I kept her busy watching me ride around on the big bass drum from the Minden High School marching band. BOOM, THUMP, BOOM, up and down the street, led by our neighbor, the band director. Then there was another exciting event. Soon after we settled in, my sister Paula was born.

One day, though, the drum rides were over. My father's work took us to live in Arkansas, and soon

Even as a young boy, I was interested in how things flew. Here I am inspecting the landing gear of my pet duck.

15

With my parents, Arnold and Frances Bean, and sister Paula.

after that, back to Fort Worth, Texas, a large city near the Brazos River. I started school there, and even though we moved once or twice more, we eventually came back. Today I still think of Fort Worth as my boyhood home.

Young people often ask me when I first got interested in traveling into space. I always have to think a little about my answer. To be honest, I don't remember one special moment. To me, it just seems as if I've always loved anything that has to do with flying.

My sister Paula doesn't look very happy being my co-pilot for the first test flight of my new kite.

There were no space travelers when I was growing up in Fort Worth, of course. And no astronaut had ever walked on the Moon. Back then, there were no astronauts—or at least not *real* ones. But there were plenty of comic books in the ten-cent store—racks and racks of stories about creepy creatures and strange planets. And the hero always traveled on a jazzy rocketship.

I loved to read. One of my favorite heroes was Buck Rogers, who was the star of a comic strip in the newspaper and in comic books called *Famous Funnies.* Buck's adventures were super-fantastic. With his cosmic-ray gun and anti-gravity jet belt—and his true friends Wilma and Dr. Huer—he always escaped from danger just in the nick of time. Usually, the villains were evil invaders from Mars. They were always strange. Once Buck even outwitted a band of robot monkeys!

In the real world there were adventures going on, too—but they were much more serious ones. When I was nine, America entered World War II. All of a sudden, newspapers and magazines were full of stories about far-off battles and the trim fighter planes flown overseas by brave pilots. In the evenings, my father talked about joining the Army Air Corps. (There was no Air Force back then.) But by the time he was able to go, he was over the age limit for pilots and had to join the regular Army instead. Not being able to become a pilot was a disappointment for Dad, but my own plans didn't change any. Even then, I think I knew that I loved airplanes more than anything else in the world. No matter what, I would be a pilot for sure.

I was a quiet boy as boys go. I wasn't an *A* student, although I liked math. It was clear-cut: Learn the rules, and you can solve all kinds of problems. But mostly my grades were *B*'s and *C*'s.

I sometimes think about those days now. I'm sure I could have done much better at school if I'd tried harder. But at the time, I had the idea that people had to be born *A* students or sports stars—that being good at things was "built-in." Whenever I wasn't great at something right away, I was sure there was no use trying to improve. Luckily, I would find out later that this attitude was wrong. With hard work, a person can be nearly anything he or she wants to be. But in those grammar school days I didn't work on spelling or geography or history. Instead, I dreamed about airplanes. If I could just find a way to fly them, that would be enough.

Outside school I had jobs to do. Mom believed that children should have jobs when they were growing up, to learn how to be responsible. No excuses were allowed: I had to work. And in those days a boy in Fort Worth could do all sorts of things. I helped the milkman deliver milk. I worked for the bakery delivering bread. For a while I helped out on Saturdays in the hardware store. And I always had a paper route.

My first route was in the early mornings. Every day was the same. I pulled myself out of my warm bed and pedaled up and down the dark streets on my bicycle, loaded with folded-up papers. It was a lonely job, too—it seemed as if there were no one else in the whole world. I always rise early now, but back then, getting up at dawn seemed just awful. After a while I changed to an afternoon route. I missed playing with my friends, but since I had to throw papers, at least I was able to do it when I was awake and when the bright Texas sun was shining.

My job situation changed during the war, when my father was off in the Army. We were living in Temple, Texas, and my mother wanted something more to do. To her, there was nothing worse than wasting time. But the "something more" she came up with was not what most mothers did in those days. She opened a grocery store!

Mom had many good qualities, and one of the best was that she was always very determined about everything she did. It never took her long to put her ideas into action. Soon she was the proud owner of the ALPA Grocery, named for ALan and PAula. And just as soon, my sister and I were under orders: we had to spend our free time sweeping floors and stocking shelves.

At this time I was starting junior high school. But had all those hours working made me forget about flying? No way—nothing could do that! My dream of becoming a pilot was stronger than ever. And I was learning a lot, too. With the war going on, books and magazines always showed pictures of different kinds of war planes. I've been lucky to have a good mind for details, and I studied those pictures by the hour. Finally, I knew each aircraft by heart—its shape and size, what kinds of stripes and symbols were painted on it, how fast it could fly.

Knowing those things gave me a new skill: from the ground I could recognize just about any plane that flew overhead. I was very proud of myself. One day, I looked up and thought I saw a German plane called a Messerschmidt ME-109. But the United States was at war with Germany; how could an enemy plane be flying over Texas? I decided that, for once, I must be wrong. Later, I learned that the military sometimes brought captured planes home and let pilots fly them to learn how they worked. So maybe the mystery plane *was* a Messerschmidt. I've never found out for sure.

The planes I knew best were much closer to home—in fact, they were "flying" in my room. They were true-to-life models of warplanes built from kits with balsa wood and glue and paints. Of course, a few—the ones that were very hard to put together—

21

sat off in a corner in a half-finished heap. But that didn't really matter much. Even as a grownup working on spacecraft, I've found that it nearly always takes a while to learn how to do something difficult.

The planes I did finish were super. Some were nifty gasoline types, with real working engines. They hung from my ceiling, like birds dressed up for a party, in shiny decals and brightly colored paints. And each one was precise. I spent hours trying to make all the details on my planes perfect. Each part had to be fitted just so. Each wing had to be exactly like the other. To me, that perfect symmetry was beautiful. I didn't care if the planes could fly, but they had to be very, very beautiful.

I bought my model airplane kits with money from my jobs. Or with some of it. Usually, I was a pack rat about money, tucking it away in some special, safe place. And I always put away something else: new clothes. Our family wasn't poor, but we were far from rich. New clothes didn't come along very often. I guess I forgot about the fact that children grow. I looked pretty silly when I had to put on a pair of new pants for a special occasion and the bottoms were up around my ankles! I'm still the same about saving things today—but at least now I don't grow any taller!

One other thing I spent money on when I was growing up was something nearly every young person likes: movies. You may not believe it, but back then, in the 1940s, the admission to a Saturday matinee was only about ten cents. The films I liked best were wartime stories about American servicemen fighting against our enemies. To me, the most exciting movies, such as *Twelve O'Clock High* and *Eagle Squadron*, were about pilots. I paid my dime, went in, and scrunched down in my seat in the dark. The screen popped and flashed with bombs dropping behind enemy lines. Then the pilot streaked through the sky, his trusty plane racing toward the safety of home. Usually the plane was full of bullet holes! When it was all over, I was exhausted. Not that I cared about bombs whistling their way down toward an enemy below. I didn't. But those soaring planes—well, you couldn't get much more exciting than that!

Before the film there was usually a newsreel. That was in the days when television had just been invented. Very few people had a TV set, and the movie newsreel showed scenes that we might see on the TV news today. Some were scenes of battlefields in Europe and the South Pacific. Others showed Navy pilots landing their fighter planes on the narrow deck of an aircraft carrier far out on the ocean. It was a very difficult maneuver. You had to be the best to do that, I thought. And it would be fun to be the best.

I was only a boy, but I think that was when I made up my mind to become a Navy pilot.

When the war ended, my father moved our family

one last time, back to Fort Worth. I was a short, skinny kid of fifteen, getting ready to enter Paschal High School. No one was surprised when my mother decided she was ready to start another business venture, too. But this time she wanted to sell something near and dear to her heart. So she bought an empty patch of land and had workers build an ice cream store.

For the next few years Paula and I took turns working after school and on Saturdays, scooping up Carnation ice cream, Mom's favorite. For customers, I fixed cones and hamburgers and sundaes. When it was slow, there was all the ice cream we could eat. The creations I remember best were banana splits with three or four scoops of vanilla ice cream and tons of fresh strawberries. Mom was a fanatic about nutrition—her children had to eat plenty of good fresh vegetables at home, and customers of Bean's Ice Cream got real strawberries!

And then—oh, boy—there were my chocolate milkshakes. They were the thickest, creamiest things. I had my own personal recipe: no milk, gobs of chocolate syrup, and a mountain of vanilla ice cream. These were beaten together S-L-O-W-L-Y on a milkshake machine until blended just right. Mmmm— those shakes were so good. I can still taste them now.

I spent a lot of hours in the store during my high school years. By then the war was over, and Dad was

Having a grand time with high school buddies Mickey Rose, Bill MacMillan, and Melvin Haas.

home. When we could, Dad took me to air shows in Grand Prairie, at the Dallas Naval Air Station. There, I saw military aircraft for real. And I watched the pilots show what skillful flyers they were. They performed loops and rolls, both solo and in close formation. Sometimes the planes flew so close together, it looked as if their wings would touch. I held my breath, but I couldn't stop looking. And when each show was over, I thought more and more about my future.

The Dallas Naval Air Station was not just a place for air shows. It had a serious purpose. People who weren't in the regular Navy could join the Air Reserve and come on weekends to train to become crewmen in a Reserve squadron. Then, in case of a national emergency, there would be a force of trained civilian pilots and crewmen. The requirements for joining were simple: A reservist had to pass a number of written tests, be healthy, of good character, and at least seventeen years old.

One summer evening I made a quiet announcement: I wanted to join the Reserve. It was a way for me to be around airplanes. If I was good, the experience might help me to become a regular Navy pilot after college and flight training. All I needed was one more birthday and permission from my parents.

It didn't go smoothly. Mom was against the whole idea. But all I could think about were those airplanes, ready and waiting. And over the years, I suppose some of my mother's determination had rubbed off on me. I was still only sixteen, but I wouldn't take no for an answer. I wrote off to Wheeler for my birth certificate, to prove my age to the Navy. I got my high school records, too. Thanks to Mom and Dad and all those years of doing jobs, I had learned how to be independent and resourceful. Pretty soon I had the mountain of paperwork all filled out.

Meanwhile, months were going by. Then March rolled around, and the day of my seventeenth birthday arrived. Mom was still worried about my decision. Finally, after some more talk, Dad gave me the best birthday present I could have asked for. He signed the papers that let me enlist in the United States Naval Air Reserve.

CHAPTER THREE

When I joined up with the Naval Air Reserve, I started to feel lucky. And when I think about it now, I was.

All new sign-ups had to take tests to show that they were physically fit. When the day came, one of the first stops was measuring weight and height. In my case I knew what the results would be; I was on the short side and skinny as a beanpole.

In school, I hated being small. I wasn't nearly as good as the bigger boys in football, where large size was important. But you can't be too big if you want to be a military pilot, because the cockpits of military planes don't have much room. For the first time in my life, I was just right—about five feet, nine inches tall. And my skinny body was strong—maybe because of all the healthy vegetables Mom had insisted on. When the physical was over, I was given a neat white uniform to wear. I felt very proud. I wasn't just a runty high school boy anymore. I was Airman Apprentice Alan Bean.

One week after I joined, my interest in airplanes paid off unexpectedly. I decided to take the exam for a higher rank, Airman Nonrated. It would be just for practice. Later on, after some training, I could take the exam for real. I had never paid much mind to tests—not in school, at least—and most of the time I didn't do better than just okay. But this day I took a test for which I seemed to know most of the answers. In fact, I passed. The test questions were mostly about airplanes and how they worked. And I had been "studying" airplanes for years.

So just like that, the skinny boy in the uniform was Airman Nonrated Alan Bean. Amazing!

Reservists did lots of different things at the Naval Air Station. We were supposed to come one weekend per month and to arrive very early on Saturday morning. The work began right away. One of my favorite jobs was getting the planes ready for the pilots to fly. The outside of a plane gets dirty, just as a car does. So I learned to wash planes and to check the fuel and oil gauges and put more in when it was needed. I learned to check the air pressure in the plane's tires. When everything was ready, I climbed up and helped the pilot get strapped into the cockpit with his shoulder harness and seat belt.

I think it's really true that time flies when you're

having fun. Those weekends at Grand Prairie went by fast. Saturday night I slept on a bunk in the barracks. On Sunday there were training classes or more work on the planes. Then, before I knew it, it was Sunday afternoon and time to go home. That was enough for most of the men in the Reserve—they were older, with jobs, families, or college work to think about. But it wasn't enough for me. Whenever I could get away from my weekend chores at Mom's store, I jumped on a bus and headed for the station.

At first, being an untrained recruit, I was not allowed to fly along with the pilot as a crew member in our squadron's airplanes. And it was hard to have to wait, because I wanted so much to fly. Then, one Saturday, the moment came.

When I arrived at the air station, my name was on the flight schedule. I was being permitted to ride in the back seat of a TBM, a World War II torpedo bomber, while an experienced pilot was at the controls. Someone handed me a parachute and showed me how to put it on. And—just in case—how to pull the cord to open it.

My stomach started to feel queasy. It was almost time to get going. I thought, I *can't* be sick—not *now*. Then I was strapped into my seat in the aircraft, and the smooth rubber wheels started rolling down the runway.

In a moment we were up, flying in formation with other aircraft from the base. But the other planes were so close! It wasn't at all what I'd thought it would be like when I'd watched at air shows. From inside the plane, flying in formation was scary. I tried to relax. I remembered how wonderful a plane looks, high up in the sky. And then, like magic, my fear turned to fun. Hey, I thought. I'm really doing this— I'm up in the air in a Navy plane!

After that first time, I did a lot of backseat flying. It was so much fun. But before long I realized that the *real* fun—flying a plane myself—was still in the future. By this time, I was starting my senior year in high school. If I wanted to become a pilot, I would need education and training. But *what* education and training? And how could I get it? The answer finally dawned on me. I knew I wanted to become a Navy pilot. So I called the Naval Recruiting officer on the phone and asked him to send me a list of the requirements for becoming a naval aviator. By the end of the year, I wanted to be as qualified as I possibly could be.

I decided that one of the best ways to become a pilot was by going to college as part of NROTC—the Naval Reserve Officer Training Corps. There was a hang-up, though. My high school grades were only average. It would be very hard for me to get into NROTC at a really good school, such as the University of Texas. Plus I had to think about money. Even with Mom's store, my family didn't have much money to pay for college.

What could I do? There was only one way I could think of for me to go to college and be in NROTC. That was to try for an NROTC scholarship. But once again, I would have to take a test and do well. Without thinking about it much, I decided that I didn't stand a chance. Also, there might be another fate in store. My reserve squadron at the air base might soon be activated into a "real" squadron and sent to fight in the war that was going on in Korea. Naturally, I would go to war, too.

I don't think I much liked the idea of going to war in a place as far away as Korea. But I have always loved my country, and I would have done my best to serve. As it happened, I didn't get the chance. Once again, my mother took the bull by the horns. And the simple thing she did changed my life.

Mom wanted me to take the NROTC scholarship test. I was stubborn. Why waste a good Saturday morning when I was bound to fail? When the day of the test came, I told her that I had the flu. Then I pulled the bedcovers up to my chin and refused to budge.

I should have known never to underestimate Mom. She was always determined to do what needed to be done. It was the only way she knew to go about life.

First she ordered me in no uncertain terms to get out of bed and get dressed. Then she went one step further. She announced that she herself was going to drive me downtown to the test center. I couldn't believe my ears. I'd always had to take care of myself. If I wanted to go somewhere, I had to take the bus or hitch a ride with a friend. Now Mom was going to drive me?

That was it. I *had* to go.

I don't remember exactly what was on the NROTC test, but many of the questions were about airplanes and flying. There was also some mathematics. I guessed that I had probably done okay—at least I wouldn't be embarrassed. But when the results came in, I was stunned. I had done *very* okay. I was a finalist and in the running for a scholarship.

Next came an interview. I wasn't sure of what to say—I have never been very good with words. So I told the officer a little bit about my life—that I was already an Airman Nonrated in the Naval Reserve and that I was flying in the backseats of airplanes every weekend. And I said I knew for sure that I wanted to go on to be a pilot. A short time later, when the list of NROTC scholarship winners was announced, my name was on it. All of a sudden, at the age of eighteen, I was a Navy midshipman on my way to college at the University of Texas!

College was a whole new world. For the first time

High school graduation.

I was completely on my own, making decisions every day. One of the first was choosing a major field of study. It can be tricky to decide something so important. Here, though, I was lucky again, because I knew exactly what I wanted. I wanted to fly airplanes, period! But at a university, there are no classes in How to Be a Pilot. For a major, the closest I could come was something called Aeronautical Engineering, a subject that has to do with the science of how airplanes fly. I knew that getting an engineering degree would be difficult, but I thought that the knowledge I would learn would help make me a better pilot. As it turned out, I was right. And something more, too. A few years later my grasp of engineering also helped me to become an astronaut.

Do you remember I said that an astronaut is an explorer? Well, in a way, I was an explorer during my first two years at college. I had so many new experiences. One of them really amazed me: as a cadet in the NROTC, I was being paid to go to school! The Navy paid for my books and college fees—and gave me fifty dollars a month for expenses. Back then, that was a lot of money. And I got a check every month in the summer, too. I couldn't believe it—so much money for just going to school!

Another new experience was being good in sports. I still had my old habit of doing as little as possible on schoolwork. That left me with time on my hands, and

I had never liked to just sit around doing nothing. Mom had seen to that. I decided to try a sport that my father had enjoyed in college: wrestling. Just as with being a pilot, in wrestling you don't have to be super-big. There are many different classes, such as middle and lightweight, for people of different sizes. I could compete in a class where my weight was just right. I began to work out hard with the wrestling team every afternoon.

Before long I was a member of the University of Texas wrestling team. Then, at a competition with another school, a strange and wonderful thing happened. I won a medal. It was for second place in my weight class, but it was the first medal I'd ever won in anything. Just as with the scholarship, I couldn't believe it. I remember thinking: This must be a mistake. A medal for me?

And more good things were just around the corner. One day after wrestling practice, I stopped to watch a group of gymnasts who were working out. I was bowled over. The gymnasts had different kinds of routines—some tumbling on floor mats, some on the parallel bars, others on the rings, twisting and turning in the air. But all of them were alike in one way: their movements were smooth and powerful. And their bodies looked strong and graceful. Before I knew it, I was thinking: *I* want to be like that.

I joined the team and started working out—hard—

doing gymnastics three or four hours every day. When the team went to meets, I won more medals. And at one of the meets I met a friendly blond tumbler named Sue. Soon we started getting together for movies and

Coming up and over the highbar for the University of Texas gymnastics team.

simple dinners. And it wasn't long before we made plans to marry after we finished college.

There were more changes taking place, too. With two years of college behind me, I still had two more to go. Up to that point, my grades had been nothing special. How could they be, when I almost never studied? Except that all of a sudden, something was happening to that "old" me.

This change didn't come from being suddenly skilled in sports, or from winning those medals as a result. It came from my realization that if I worked hard, I would get better. At the end of each day's practice, I couldn't see any improvement. However, after several months of practice, I could do things I couldn't do before. And after several years, I was no longer trying to be a wrestler—I *was* a wrestler.

So I started to listen more in class and to use my time differently. I did my homework. The results were good grades for the first time in my life. And do you know what? Just the way it happens in cartoons, a little light blinked on inside my head. I started to understand that there's no such thing as being born a "superstar." No, the answer to my old "problem" of how to do better was not that I needed to be born smarter. The answer lay in working hard.

That was the most important lesson I learned in college. I know that without it, I never could have gone on to do many of the things I have done in my life. I learned that it was important to plan, too—and to be ready to make changes. I like to tell young people—like you—to always keep moving in the direction of their dreams. In the beginning, you may not know how to achieve your goals. By taking the first steps toward them you will discover what steps to take next. The most important thing is never to let up. If you don't know what you did yesterday, or plan to do today, to achieve your dreams, you never will. And one thing will never change—you'll always have to work hard.

In January 1955, at the age of twenty-two, I graduated from the University of Texas with a Bachelor of Science degree in aeronautical engineering. Sue and I were married, and I was commissioned as an ensign in the Navy. I was ordered to Pensacola, Florida, to begin my flight training. I was finally going to have a chance to make my boyhood dream come true. But as it turned out, becoming a real Navy pilot was not the end of anything. It was the beginning of a whole new chapter of my life.

CHAPTER FOUR

You might think that learning to fly an airplane is easy—that fancy instruments do all the work and the pilot has all the fun. And you would be right about one thing: Fighter jets built today have powerful computers. But even with a cockpit full of dials and buttons and gauges, the most important "computer" is the pilot. When I arrived at the Navy training center in Pensacola, Florida, I discovered how much there was for a pilot to learn. I had to be thinking every single minute.

My work started with school. For hours, I sat in a classroom to learn how to start the plane's engine, how to taxi on the runway, how to take off and land. My head buzzed. There was so much to remember! Afterward, there were written tests on every step. And always there were days when I had to take facts I'd learned in books or in the classroom and put them to work in a real airplane. In the beginning, I always flew with an instructor. But it wasn't like being in the

Naval Air Reserve. Now, when the plane rolled down the runway, I was in the pilot's seat.

Each flight began with a pre-flight briefing by the flight instructor. He would go over in great detail what we planned to practice during the flight. When he was satisfied that I understood what he had in mind, we picked up our parachutes and went out to the line shack. There we would read the yellow sheet, a booklet that contained the recent history of the airplane. Then we walked out to the airplane to do our "preflight check." That means taking a slow, careful walk around the plane, asking a headful of questions. Are the tires fit for flight? Do they have any cuts or knicks that would make them unsafe? Are the wheel nuts on tightly? Do all the control surfaces move smoothly? There were dozens more questions, and it was important to ask each one. Finally, we made a personal check that the gas and oil were okay.

Every day at Pensacola, I was learning tons and tons of things. And every time I went flying with an instructor, I became a little bit better pilot. Finally, it was the day of my first solo flight—the first time I would fly a plane all by myself. With my instructor, I had practiced all the moves over and over. I thought I could do it. Just to make sure, a new instructor climbed into the backseat of my plane. Quietly, watching and listening, he rode along while I did trial runs—takeoff and land, takeoff and land. My landings were a little bumpy—that's always the hardest part of flying. But after the second practice run, the new instructor folded up the backseat and jumped out onto the airfield.

I heard the words "Good luck" and started rolling. My heart was thumping, like the big bass drum all those years ago in Minden. But not from fear. I knew that if I could use the knowledge from my studies and all those hours of practicing, I would do all right. I just want to do it right, I thought. That's all.

Three times I went up, landed, and went up again. The last time I landed, I picked up the instructor, and we flew back to the base. That was it—I had soloed. I was a real pilot at last.

But my solo flight was just a beginning. On top of practicing basics, such as takeoffs and landings, I had to spend a whole year learning how to do acrobatic loops and rolls, how to navigate and fly on instruments alone, and how to fly in formation with other planes. The next step was a trip to a little Texas town called Beeville, for advance training on high-performance jets. My days were spent practicing bombing runs and strafing and other skills—things that I'd need to be able to do if I ever had to fly in defense of my country.

At the end of my training I had officially earned my wings as a Navy aviator. I still remember the ceremony on an early June afternoon in Beeville. And I

It's official! Mom pinning Naval aviator wings to my uniform.

remember how proud I was when Mom and Dad arrived, and when Mom pinned the shiny gold aviator's wings on my uniform.

It was a time in my life when lots of things were changing. One change was a wonderful, small bundle in a blue blanket: Sue and I had a son. We named him Clay and gave him the middle name of Arnold, after my father. I also got my new orders from the Navy: I was to be a pilot with Attack Squadron 44, based at the Naval Air Station in Jacksonville, Florida.

The squadron's job was to be prepared to fight an enemy from the air if there ever should be a war. Back then, that meant dropping nuclear bombs. It was something we hoped we would never have to do, and of course we didn't. But just in case, it was important for our country that the Navy be ready. And even though the mission of our squadron was serious, I loved what I was doing. Every day I was flying. Some days I practiced flying very close to the ground—not much higher than the roof of a house. That was to learn to evade enemy radar. At other times my job for the day was bombing target practice.

Every once in a while I took a special kind of trip and flew my jet out over the blue ocean waves, to a waiting Navy aircraft carrier. That's a ship with an unusually long, open deck. It is like an airfield at sea. Then, while the ship traveled to different places, I practiced taking off and landing on it. Carrier landings are very difficult because there isn't much room for

As a member of Attack Squadron 44.

error. I had to learn to be very precise.

The hardest part is bringing the plane in so a hook at the back of the plane catches a steel cable that's stretched across the ship's deck. The cable is attached to a device that works like the shock absorber of a car. It's supposed to slow down the plane quickly and smoothly, so it can come to a stop before it reaches the end of the ship's deck. There are several cables, and the plane's hook only has to catch onto one of them. But the airplane it has to catch is traveling very fast, at a speed of 150 knots. That's about 170 miles per hour!

What happens if the pilot misjudges and the hook misses the cable? Well, if the plane is too high, the pilot will touch down, power up again, and circle around for another try. If the plane is too low, an officer on deck will signal to the pilot to try again. Otherwise the plane's nose might wind up sticking into the end of the ship! But all pilots want to catch the cable on the first try if they can.

I traveled to many places on aircraft carriers—to the sunny Caribbean, to rainy Scotland, even to the icy waters of the Arctic. Always, I was trying to improve my skills as a pilot so that if my country ever needed me I'd be able to do the job. But after a while I found myself thinking: Yes, I have become a very good pilot, but where do I go from here? How can I be better?

Part of being a good pilot—or a good anything—is knowing *how* to be good. I began to realize it was not enough just to know the facts I had learned in school. I had to begin to direct my efforts to make my dreams come true. Schools don't teach you how to do that sort of thing. I needed to figure out what new things to learn, what old things to practice.

But where could I look for this how-to stuff? The answer may surprise you, but it was simple, once I discovered it—in the self-help section of bookstores. Most self-help books provide techniques for solving a problem or reaching a specific goal. The first one I read, when I had only just become a real pilot, was *Think and Grow Rich,* by Napoleon Hill. Now, I didn't want to be rich, but I did want to be a great naval aviator. Maybe I could "think and grow great" by using some of the principles in that book. Over the next ten years, self-help books helped me see the specific things I needed to do to make my dreams come true. If you have a dream, I think reading self-help books is one of the best pieces of advice I could give you.

When I started looking for a way to be a better pilot, it didn't take long to find the answer. I knew that some of the most challenging work for a pilot was flying and testing different kinds of new planes—planes that could go faster and higher than any others. The work of a test pilot could also be dangerous. The new planes were complicated, and no one knew how they would work under different conditions. I thought about the danger. But I couldn't help thinking something else. Being a test pilot, I would improve my skills as an aviator. I would help develop the kinds of planes the Navy of the future would need. And for sure, I would have a ton of fun. So, when my tour with the attack squadron was nearly over, I applied to the U.S. Navy Test Pilot School in Patuxent River, Maryland. Or just Pax River, for short.

I was twenty-eight, and the year was 1960. Before long, in April of 1961, Yuri Gargarin would make his historic trip into space as the world's first astronaut. Then it would be Alan Shepard's turn. Shepard had once been a test pilot at Pax River. Getting into Pax River was always very competitive, but I thought that my background of flying light attack planes might help me. It did. Several months later I received a letter saying I had been selected. And as it would turn out, being at Pax would make all the difference in my own future as an astronaut.

First I had eight months of basic test pilot training. Then I received my assignment to a test group—I was to work in a unit called Service Test. Right away I was given a job I didn't like. It had to do with—of all things—ejection seats.

The ejection seat is part of a plane's safety system: when there is trouble, it lets a pilot escape from a plane and parachute safely to earth. But, with nobody knowing it, trouble can start on the ground. So, every so often, mechanics took each test plane apart for servicing and then put it back together. And though they did their best at a complicated job, sometimes an ejection seat would be reassembled incorrectly. As a result, good test pilots sometimes died.

It was a tragic puzzle. There were lots of different kinds of planes being tested. And many had ejection seats that looked very different from others. How could a pilot know whether the seat was properly rigged before he climbed in and flew?

No one had had much luck in trying to solve the puzzle. Then it was handed over to me. Even though I didn't want the job, I knew that the best way to succeed was to have a good attitude about it. I made up my mind to find a way to enjoy what had to be done, and to give it my best effort. I had also been given command of a division—about a hundred men— and I needed to learn how to be a leader. But could I find a way to save lives at the same time?

My first step was to do some basic learning. I read every book on ejection seats I could get my hands on. I talked with technical experts. (There's always a lot of knowledge around, if you're willing to look for it.) Every time I thought I had a solution, one of the experts would explain to me why my idea wouldn't work. But I kept plugging. No one can expect to succeed at something difficult the very first time. I knew

I would fail at first, but through failing I would learn new information. Slowly, facts and ideas started coming together. And after lots of tries and misses, I finally found the answer I was looking for.

All ejection seats must have parts that do the same important jobs. Just the way that different kinds of cars must all have something to make the cars go, something to make them stop, and something for the drivers to steer with. Once I learned what the main parts of an ejection seat were, I made a checklist. Then I showed the checklist to all the pilots in Service Test. The list told them how to find the basic parts in any seat and how to make sure each one was rigged properly.

Later I was asked to do the same thing with pilots in other test units, too. I was nervous about getting up and speaking about my new ideas. But I did okay, and the pilots put the system to use. Of course, for a while I worried every day that something would go wrong with an ejection seat. But it never did. There were no more ejection seat tragedies. Today, when I look back, I still feel very satisfied about having helped to solve that puzzle.

But the main job of a test pilot is to fly airplanes. And I did plenty of that.

Some people might say that a test pilot's job is to take chances. In a way that is true. Usually, though, I didn't dwell on the risks of being a test pilot—and anyway, the excitement and adventure were worth it. The planes I was testing were small and fast and maneuverable—they could shoot up into the clouds, whip along just above the treetops, or drop down over a target with lightning speed. Every second, I had to watch, listen, concentrate. Did the controls seem to be working properly? Could the plane do all the things another pilot would need it to do on a real mission? There wasn't much time to think of danger. Instead, those were busy and happy days.

But I do remember one scary flying adventure. It happened at night, in a thunderstorm. Pilots at Pax River had to test-fly planes in bad weather, to make sure the plane could perform even when skies were stormy. That meant finding the biggest thunderstorms and flying through them.

I was storm-testing a nifty little plane, called the A4-E Skyhawk. Every flight, I squeezed down in my seat as far as I could go. I hoped that I wouldn't be hit by the lightning bolts that came crashing through the clouds. Sometimes, when I landed, I saw that lightning had blown off my plane's radio antennas, or shattered its nose cone to pieces. Always, there was damage to repair. Of course, I acted very cool about the whole thing—as if being struck by lightning happened every day. Then, one afternoon, the repairs on my plane took so long that it wasn't ready on time. I could have waited and taken it out the next morning.

But instead I decided to go up that evening, in the dark.

I climbed into the Skyhawk, scrunched down, and headed up toward the center of a storm. Gray-black clouds closed around my little plane. Raindrops pounded like bullets against its thin metal skin. Then the lightning started. *Flash! Crack!* Every time the plane was hit, it shuddered and shook. In the daytime, you don't see all the lightning bolts. But that night in the dark, lightning seemed to be everywhere at once. All of a sudden I didn't feel quite so cool. I pulled back on the throttle, turned the plane away from the storm, and circled back to the airfield. When I landed and stepped out of the Skyhawk, for once I was glad to be on the ground instead of in the air. In all my flying, I had never been so scared. I never flew into a thunderstorm at night again—at least, not on *purpose!*

Most of my evenings during those test pilot years were much quieter, but they were busy. As much as possible, I spent time with my family. I also started something new: night school classes in art. Not many test pilots did artistic things in their spare time. But I didn't think it was strange. I had always loved anything that looked beautiful—a perfectly built airplane, a graceful gymnast. And I'd always liked to make things. When I moved my family into our first little house in Jacksonville, I made a lot of our furniture and sewed drapes for the windows.

Plus, the classes were fun. In one, I made a picture using glue and tiny bits of green-tinted glass. The design was very streamlined, like a V on its side, with a tip like the nose of an airplane. I called my creation "The Spirit of Flight." Later on, when I became an astronaut, I turned the V on end, so that it pointed up like a rocket ship. It still hangs that way in my house today.

When I took those first art classes I had no idea that painting—including scenes from my own trip to the Moon—would one day become a very important part of my life. Exciting things were happening. In 1959, during my last year as a pilot in Jacksonville, the first American astronauts, the Mercury Seven, had been chosen. All of them were test pilots. In 1962, when I had completed my training and was a test pilot at Pax River, NASA announced that America needed a second group of space explorers. With my college degree in aeronautical engineering and two years of test pilot training, I had all of the basic qualifications. All of a sudden, I had a brand-new dream.

Right away, I applied. Of the thousands of applicants, I made the final group of thirty-five. When the new astronaut group was named, though, Alan Bean wasn't on the list. I was very disappointed. But then I started thinking about some of the lessons I'd learned about working hard and persevering. NASA officials had chosen the applicants they thought were most qualified. And the space program was growing—America would soon need even more astronauts. I still had a chance. But if I wanted to be selected, I would have to do everything I could to make sure that next time *I* was "most qualified."

Once more, I began to read every book I could find—books on space flight and rockets and astronomy. Every day I worked out to keep physically fit. And I did the best job I could as a pilot, so that my recommendations would be good.

Then, one bright June day in 1963, I learned that NASA was calling for a third group of astronaut candidates. Some of those chosen would be trained for the Apollo program—the one that would take mankind to the Moon. My test pilot training was over, and I was stationed at Cecil Field, Florida, as part of Attack Squadron 172. When I heard the news, I didn't have to think twice. I had done everything I could to be ready. I got the forms to fill out and applied again.

This time even more people wanted to become members of the corps of astronauts. Soon NASA announced that thirty-two finalists—including me—would go to Texas for medical tests. I went, wondering what my fate would be. Then, one afternoon in October, I was working in my backyard when the telephone rang. It was Deke Slayton, chief astronaut at NASA, saying that fourteen new astronauts had been selected. And one of them was me.

CHAPTER FIVE

Have you ever been so excited about something that you thought about it nearly every waking minute? Well, that's how it was for me that warm autumn morning when the telephone call came from NASA. Once more, with lots of hard work and a shot of luck, a dream was coming true.

The headquarters for astronaut training was the Manned Spacecraft Center in Houston, Texas. Soon, I moved there with my family—including a new, smiling little baby girl, my daughter Amy. But even though I was officially an astronaut, I didn't put on a space suit and climb into a spacecraft right away. In fact, six whole years were to pass before my time would come. It was very hard to be patient all those years. But while I waited—and wondered when I would go into space—there was plenty to keep me busy.

First, I had basic training. That meant learning all about rocket engines and studying astronomy. And because astronauts-in-training might one day visit the

On the backyard swing in Jacksonville, Florida, with son Clay, newborn daughter Amy, and Richelieu, the pup.

Moon, we also had to learn geology. I traveled to a lot of places, including parts of Iceland and Hawaii, that scientists thought in some ways might be like the Moon. On those trips I learned how to look at rocks and hills and mountains the way a geologist does. Why? Well, if I ever set foot on the Moon, I would be trained to collect useful materials for geologists on Earth to study. By studying rocks and soil from the Moon, they might gain very important knowledge about the Earth, too.

Just like today's astronauts, part of my job was to become expert in one special area. My specialty was Spacecraft Recovery Systems. I had to help plan the methods that would be used to bring a spacecraft and its crew safely back to Earth, to a jolting splashdown in the ocean, where they could be picked up by a Navy ship. I also had to spend time flying jets to keep my pilot's skills sharp. At the end of basic training I received a little silver pin. It meant that I was a full-fledged astronaut.

To carry out a successful space flight, many people—scientists, engineers, astronauts—have to plan and work very carefully and for a very long time. When I first joined the corps of astronauts, the planners were working on two big programs. In one of them, I hoped, I would get my chance for space travel. The first program, called Project Gemini, was planned for ten missions. The Gemini astronauts would learn how to do tricky maneuvers, such as bringing two spacecraft very near to each other in space, then docking them together. On Earth, scientists would study how being in space for more than just a few hours affected the human body. And at least one lucky Gemini astronaut would become the first American to "walk" in space.

Gemini sounded great. But there was an even more exciting project. It would come after Gemini and be named Apollo. At least some Apollo missions would go to the Moon. That sounded wonderful. The Apollo program would be one of the greatest space adventures of all.

There were dozens of astronauts, and I knew that only some could be chosen for Apollo. More than any-

Inside the Kennedy Space Center's Flight Crew Training building. Pete and I are simulating photographic documentation of lunar rock samples.

thing, I wanted to be one of them. Meanwhile, I was assigned to work on Gemini—to train to do the countdown on launch day and call the lift-off. That mission brought two spacecraft, *Gemini 6* and *Gemini 7,* into orbit side by side. It was a difficult and important step in our progress toward later Moon missions. Six months later I was chosen to be backup commander for another flight, *Gemini 10.* On that mission, astronaut Michael Collins made two "walks" in space, floating outside the spacecraft at the end of a special cable.

More time went by. While other astronauts were being selected for spaceflights, I was still waiting. I did have plenty to do—for the *Gemini 11* flight, in September, 1966, I was capcom—the person who talks over the radio to astronauts in space. But nothing really *wonderful* was happening to me. Then, when the *Gemini 11* capsule, with astronauts Pete Conrad and Dick Gordon, had completed its mission and splashed safely into the Atlantic Ocean, I received some news. But not the kind I was hoping for. I was to be given a new assignment as chief of the Apollo Applications Office. It was a long-term job to plan for making an orbiting space station out of the Apollo spacecraft. The space station would be called Skylab, and I'll tell you more about its important work later. But the assignment meant I would sit behind a desk. There would be no time to train for a flight into space.

Just like that, my dream of becoming a real "sailor to the stars" seemed to be over.

I was awfully disappointed. But it wasn't the first time in my life something hadn't gone the way it was "supposed" to. I would have to find a way to make this assignment interesting. Though it was tough and I hurt a lot, I would be the best chief of Apollo Applications I could be.

A whole year of working went by. Apollo flight crews were chosen, with no Alan Bean among them. Every time the names were announced, my heart broke a little. Then Pete Conrad, who was one of my teachers at test-pilot school in Pax River, was selected to command a future Apollo mission. Conrad and his crew might orbit the Earth when they went into space, or they might be chosen to go all the way to the Moon. I tried not to think about it. My job, I told myself, was to concentrate on Skylab.

One afternoon I decided to take a jet up to spend a few hours flying. I was keeping my skills sharp, just in case. And flying was always fun. When I arrived at the airfield, Pete Conrad was there, and for a moment I couldn't help thinking: Lucky Pete, going into space on Apollo! I wasn't expecting anything when I saw him—just a friendly hello. I didn't know that Pete had something else in mind.

Pete asked if he could speak to me for a moment. Sure, I said. Quietly, my old teacher asked if I would

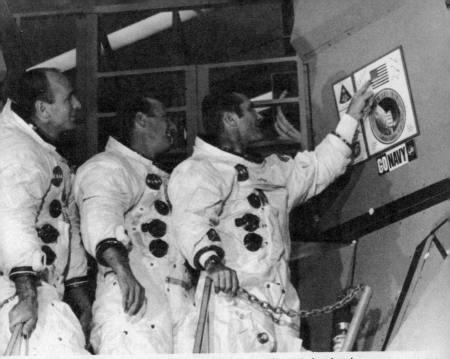

*Pete, Dick, and I looking at the Apollo 12 insignia on
the Command Module Mission Simulator.*

like to be part of his Apollo crew. The job he had in
mind for me was pilot of the Lunar Module—the small
craft that would separate from the Command Module
and take two astronauts down to the surface of the
Moon.

I couldn't believe my ears. Pete said he had talked
with head astronaut Deke Slayton and had asked for
me. Deke had said okay. I don't remember exactly
what *I* said, but it must have been yes. It was so
amazing—finally, my dream was coming true.

61

Soon, NASA announced that our Apollo flight would go to the Moon. First, though, Pete, Dick, and I were the backup crew for another mission. That was Apollo 9, which spent ten days in orbit around the Earth. It was a very important mission: a practice for many of the difficult tasks men and machines would have to do when we finally went to the Moon.

After another mission—Apollo 10—which flew to within ten miles of the Moon, the historic moment came for all mankind. The astronauts of Apollo 11 made the first manned landing on the Moon. Commander Neil Armstrong became the first human to set foot on the lunar surface, and Lunar Module pilot Edwin Aldrin became the second. They "moonwalked" for two hours, exploring the rocky, dusty world where no person had ever gone before. And when the Apollo 11 astronauts came home to Earth, the whole world was proud.

The first Moon landing happened on July 20, 1969. Four months later, early on a rainy November morning, a thundering Saturn rocket lifted off a Florida launchpad. It carried the astronauts of Apollo 12, speeding on their way toward the second manned visit to the Moon. Inside the Command Module atop the rocket, I lay strapped to my couch. I was going into space at last.

CHAPTER SIX

When I think back to my Apollo days, I remember their being busy. Every minute was filled with work—training, practicing, preparing. And I remember those days as being happy. But, of course, one of the surest ways to be happy in life is to work at a job you love. And I was loving every second of being an Apollo astronaut.

As usual, the Apollo 12 mission was planned very carefully. It had to be, because every minute we spent on the Moon was going to cost millions of dollars! In all, Pete Conrad and I—and our little Lunar Module, *Intrepid*—would spend thirty-one hours on the Moon's surface. Pete and I would set up instruments for five scientific experiments. We would moonwalk for more than seven hours, collecting samples of soil and rocks. We would also try to make our way to a previous Moon visitor, called *Surveyor*. *Surveyor* was an unmanned spacecraft. Carrying a television camera and an automated digger, it had been sent to the Moon

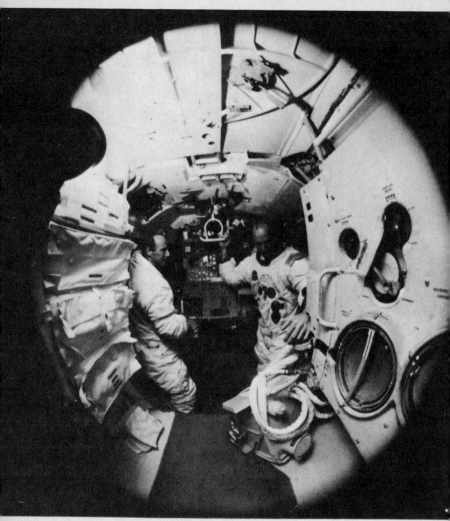

A fish-eye lens view of Pete and me inside the Lunar Module Mission Simulator during training.

almost three years earlier. Meanwhile, Dick Gordon would be in charge of *Yankee Clipper*—the Command Module that would orbit the Moon, waiting for us to return.

Launch day was November 14, 1969. That morning the weather was gloomy. During the night, rain had pelted the launch area from thick, dark clouds. More rain was expected. But even in bad weather everything was as ready as it could be. The huge Saturn rocket that would lift *Yankee Clipper* and *Intrepid* into space was waiting on its launchpad at Cape Kennedy, Florida. Pete, Dick, and I woke up early and ate a big breakfast: steak, eggs, toast, coffee, and orange juice. Then each of us climbed into a bulky space suit and put on a snug-fitting cap with a radio microphone wired into it. Last of all came a hard plastic helmet. Soon we were on our way to the waiting rocket.

In the Command Module—the capsule where Apollo astronauts lived and worked while in space— we slipped onto our couches and strapped ourselves in. I was responsible for the spacecraft's electrical and communication systems. In front of me were switches and lights and indicators—in all, there were more than seven hundred of them, connected to sixteen miles of electrical wiring, in the spacecraft. I kept a constant watch on the control panel. As the final minutes went by, my heart beat faster and faster. Outside and far below, scientists at the launch center worried about

Suiting up for my first trip as a sailor to the stars!

the rain: Was it bad enough to cancel the launch? Finally, the decision was made. No one thought the rainstorm would cause any harm. The answer was GO.

I heard and felt the Saturn V rocket—the largest rocket in the world—roar into action. The Command Module trembled and shook. Slowly, our rocket ship, with its cargo of astronauts and spacecraft, began to rise through the clouds. Rain or no rain, I was on my way into space.

But if I thought my first space adventure would get off to a smooth start, I was wrong.

The first problem came almost at once. Thirty-six seconds after the lift-off and a mile up, it happened: Just outside the Command Module windows, there was a brilliant streak of light. Instantly, yellow caution lights and red warning lights on the control panel in front of me flashed on. Then Pete was calling out the warning lights and talking over the radio with the capcom on the ground. Somehow, the fuel cells that gave electrical power to the spacecraft had been disconnected. And that wasn't all. Our guidance platform, instruments we would need to navigate to the Moon, was knocked out, too. But by what?

Meanwhile, the Saturn V was still roaring upward. That was good. It meant that whatever happened, we were still going where we wanted to go—up. There was no need for panic—only cool, solid thinking. We waited for "staging," the moment when the fuel in the first stage of the Saturn rocket would be used up and the stage would plummet to the ocean below. It went according to plan. Then, after talking with the ground, one at a time I pushed switches that would reset the fuel cells. If turning them back on was the wrong decision, I wanted to find out before I had done them all.

But as I flipped the switches, nothing else went wrong. Instead, warning lights began to blink off. And we had an idea about what had happened. Maybe, Pete suggested, we had been hit by lightning from the rainstorm.

That guess turned out to be exactly right. Lightning had struck the Command Module as it traveled up through the storm. Luckily, the powerful Saturn rocket had kept right on pushing us out of the storm and up toward the heavens. And it had all happened so fast, there hadn't even been time to be scared.

Our four-day journey to the Moon would take us through 239,000 miles of space. But first we had to orbit twice around the Earth and take care of some business. And because of the lightning, we had to get the guidance system working properly again so that it could guide us when the Saturn rocket finally pushed us out toward the moon.

When we reached Earth orbit I felt weightlessness for the first time. At first, weightlessness is pleasant—

I felt the way I do when I'm floating in a swimming pool. My 150-pound body seemed feather-light. I could float around the spacecraft by just pushing off in the direction I wanted to go. I'll tell you a lot more about weightlessness, and about living in space, in the next chapter.

Finally the Saturn rocket fired one last time and pushed *Yankee Clipper* and *Intrepid* out of Earth orbit and onto the path to the Moon.

Now it was time to turn the Command Module around to dock with the Lunar Module. As we swung around, I saw the most incredible sight I've ever seen. Can you guess what it was? I looked out my window and saw the Earth. It hung in the black of space, already very far away. Maybe you have seen beautiful pictures of our planet taken from spacecraft. Those pictures are nice. But nothing could compare to seeing Earth from space with my own eyes. It was so hard to believe that my family and friends—in fact, everyone in the whole world except Dick, Pete, and me—was down there on that lovely blue and white ball. After we had docked with the Lunar Module, we pulled *Intrepid* away from the spent Saturn 5 so that we could continue our journey. Time went by. We traveled closer and closer to the Moon. Then, three days and twelve hours after the lift-off, we were nearly there. With little *Intrepid* attached, *Yankee Clipper* slipped behind the edge of the Moon. We fired its engine to slow our speed. When the engine shut off, we were safely in orbit around the Moon. After three orbits, Pete and Dick got into sleeping bags and strapped themselves into their couches. I crawled into my bag *under* my couch—in zero gravity, that's where I could sleep the best. Then we settled in for a few hours' sleep. When we woke up, it would be time to land.

In the first chapter of this book I told you a little of what it was like bringing *Intrepid* to rest on the Moon. Our landing—only the second one in history—came on November 19, 1969. We planned to land in a place called the Ocean of Storms, near a crater where the *Surveyor* craft had landed months earlier. To do that, we needed to find a landmark: a group of three Moon craters called Snowman. *Surveyor* was in Snowman's belly, off to one side.

Pete and I put on our moon suits, said good-bye to Dick Gordon, and moved through a tunnel into *Intrepid*. We prepared the Lunar Module for undocking and landing. Then Dick Gordon closed the hatches and we were ready to go.

After several orbits we began our descent to the surface of the Moon. I watched the radar as we came closer and closer. Whenever I could, I sneaked a look out my window. The view—all those craters, craters everywhere—was incredible. Even though I was very busy, every once in a while a thought flashed through my mind! In a moment, I would really be on the Moon! Finally, with a solid thump, we touched down right on the edge of the crater where *Surveyor* had landed months before. We had flown nearly a quarter of a million miles in a spaceship and come in for a pinpoint landing!

At last we were on the Moon. I felt fine—but how was our spaceship doing? Had it sprung a leak? Was the electrical system okay? Pete and I, together with the flight controllers in Houston, performed a number of checks on critical systems. At last we all breathed a sigh of relief. Everything was perfect.

As eager as tourists, we finally allowed ourselves a brief look out the window. Then we began to power down *Intrepid,* got ourselves some lunch, and put our backpacks on. We were ready to perform the experiments we had come so far to do.

Pete was the first to step down *Intrepid*'s ladder onto the lunar surface. Right away, he gathered a sample of soil and rock, put them into a bag, and sent the bag up to me on a sort of rope-and-pulley. We did that so even if something happened and we had to leave the Moon in a hurry, we would have some material for scientists to study.

Next it was my turn to go down. At first, I needed to get used to Moon gravity, so I could move about without falling down. Lunar gravity is one-sixth as strong as the Earth's. At home in Houston, I would have weighed 300 pounds in my moon suit. Now, my suit and I were only fifty pounds.

What did I feel during those first moments on the Moon? Well, I was excited. And I remember thinking, just for a second: Wow! I'm on the Moon, and that's the Earth way out there! But then I caught myself. There was so much that scientists back on Earth wanted to learn about the Moon. Our mission was full of useful work that needed to be done. There'd be time later for thinking about the wonder of being a man on the Moon.

In the bright Moon morning, Pete and I got right to work. First, I checked *Intrepid,* to make sure that it hadn't been damaged during the landing. Then we unpacked experiments and set them up. Everything we did kicked up powdery, grayish dust. Pete and I planted the American flag. Next we set up the instruments in the ALSEP—the Apollo Lunar Surface Experiments Package—including a seismometer to measure meteorite impacts and moonquakes.

The seismometer was very sensitive. It even recorded our footsteps as we walked on the lunar surface. And by now, we could move very well, although not the same way we did on Earth. My space suit was very hard to move in the hip and knee joints but easier to move in the ankle joint. I enjoyed tiptoeing along, like a ballet dancer or a little boy taking a secret

One of my first extravehicular activities on the Moon: unpacking equipment from the Modular Equipment Stowage Assembly on the outside of the Lunar Module. [NASA]

look at his Christmas presents. And I was able to run and never get tired.

My suit also included a backpack—the life-support system tht gave me oxygen to breathe and helped keep the inside of my moon suit cool. You see, there is no oxygen on the Moon. My suit was pressurized, which helped the oxygen molecules flow into my lungs. On Earth, normal air-pressure from our atmosphere does that. What would happen if I hadn't worn a moon suit, or if my suit had sprung a leak? I wouldn't have exploded, or anything like that. But in an instant I would have fallen unconscious. And in a few minutes I would have died.

Once the ALSEP experiments were in place, our next job was to gather more rock and soil samples. Every now and then, I glanced at the far-off Earth, so busy with living things—dogs and cats, trees and people. On the Moon, except for the *whirr* of my life-support pack and voices coming now and then over the radio, all was silent. Outside my suit, just inches away, there was no sound, because there was no air to carry it. And there was nothing to chirp or bark or even move.

After almost four hours of work, we headed back to *Intrepid* for a meal and a rest. We were both hungry and tired. I was looking forward to my favorite meal—spaghetti. Like most "space food" in those days, it tasted pretty bland. But I didn't care much about that.

I have photographed Pete Conrad as he sets out one of the experiments of the Apollo Lunar Surface Experiments Package (ALSEP). [NASA]

I had told my children, Clay and Amy, that their dad was going to be the first man to eat spaghetti on the Moon. And I was.

Then Pete and I cleaned up, crawled into our hammocks, and fell asleep.

Nine hours later, we suited up again, checked out the spacecraft, ate breakfast, and got ready for our second moonwalk.

This time, we would do lots more geology and collect as many kinds of moon rocks as we could find in different sizes and shapes. We were also supposed to take samples of dirt from different places. And we were supposed to take pictures of *Surveyor* and remove the TV camera. Along with the rocks, we would bring these things back to Earth for scientists to study.

It was exciting work to poke around in craters and explore the dusty, lifeless world of the Moon. Using special tongs, I collected small rocks. Pete saw one he particularly liked—it was big and sort of round and made him think of a grapefruit. We brought that one back, too.

Using the radio built into my headgear, I reported my observations to Earth. I especially noticed shapes and colors. On the first walk we had seen chest-high mounds, piled up like baby volcanoes. They turned out to be only clumps of dirt. And this time I noticed little white craters with white rims. There were big, chunky rocks and little ones too, all pitted with small

I pose for a photograph after taking a soil sample using the small scoop in my right hand. [NASA]

craters over their surfaces. Some rocks were made shiny by a coating of glass. Some craters seemed to have little glass beads jumbled at the bottoms of their hollows. And everywhere were the colors of the Moon: mousy brown here, dusty tan over there, steely cement-gray a few inches down in the dirt.

Finally, after visiting *Surveyor,* it was time to head back to *Intrepid.* On the way, we collected more rock samples and took pictures. I was thirsty and tired—especially in my hands, because it's hard to grasp things in moon gloves. I was happy and satisfied, too. We had a long way to go before we were safely home again, but I knew we had done our moon jobs well.

Back inside *Intrepid* we stowed our gear, packed the precious samples of rock and soil, and cleaned up the cabin as much as we could. That wasn't easy, because there was moon dust everywhere. We were worried about going home to Earth with dangerous germs that might be in the dust, but there was nothing we could do. As it turned out, the scientists found no signs of germs or any life at all in the things we brought back. But we had to be careful, just the same.

Finally, it was time to leave. Dick Gordon was orbiting sixty miles above us in *Yankee Clipper,* waiting for our return. Exactly thirty-one hours and thirty-one minutes after *Intrepid* came to rest on the Moon, the little module's ascent stage—the engine that would carry us up to *Yankee Clipper*—started with a loud bang. Then, just like a super-fast, quiet elevator ride, we were up and away.

Three hours later we met up with *Yankee Clipper* and docked. When all of our gear and samples were safely aboard, *Intrepid* was sent crashing down onto the Moon. The crash was an experiment, to be measured by the seismometer we had left behind. And I guess *Intrepid* hit hard. Scientists watching instruments in Houston said that when the little Lunar Module hit, the Moon rang like a bell.

That experiment told a great deal about the inner structure of the moon. And in the years since Apollo, researchers studying the rock and soil samples have learned that the Moon is very much like the Earth in some ways. But they have also learned that, in other ways, it is very *different* from the Earth. Today, scientists are still working to discover the reasons why.

On the four-day return trip in *Yankee Clipper,* I spent a lot of time sleeping. And some time thinking, too. Exploring the Moon had been the most fantastic adventure ever. And standing there—on that dusty, rocky place—I had looked back at the blue Earth and thought: How very beautiful our Earth is. I'd been so lucky to go to the Moon. But after all was said and done, I was also very glad to be going home.

Fort Worth, Texas welcomed us home with a glorious ticker-tape parade!

CHAPTER SEVEN

For me, the best part of going into space was having a chance to perform at my best in work worth doing. And seeing so many wonderful sights. It was amazing to look out the window of a spaceship—or to stand on the Moon—and see the Earth as a lovely blue and white ball. I was also surprised when I looked at the Moon. It is much smaller than Earth, of course. But I discovered that the Moon looks little, even up close. When I was in orbit and peered out the window, I felt that if I could stretch up a little farther in my seat, I would be able to see all the way around it!

On my second trip into space I was commander of an exciting mission: to live and work in Skylab, America's first space station. Skylab circled the Earth in an orbit 270 miles high. My mission would be only the second time it was visited by astronauts. Our Skylab visit would last for fifty-nine days. At the time, it was the longest manned journey into space.

On the morning of July 28, 1973, more than thirty-

Training for Skylab III in the Neutral Buoyancy Tank.

five thousand people were watching as a Saturn rocket lifted me and my crew—astronauts Owen Garriott and Jack Lousma—up toward Skylab through a gray morning sky. What had all those people come to see? Well, the noise, fire, and vibration of a rocket launch will give anybody goose bumps. If you ever have a chance to see a launch in person, you should do it.

Skylab was a real space station. In its orbit high above the Earth, it had everything we would need to live and work in space for a long time. There was a workshop for scientific experiments and equipment for medical tests. There were bunks for sleeping, a kitchen area, and a bathroom with toilet facilities and a shower. There were compartments to hold our clothes, books to read, and music tapes to listen to. There was even a vacuum cleaner so we could do "housework." (Usually, that ended up being my job!) After docking with Skylab, Owen, Jack, and I spent several days unpacking and getting our new home shipshape. When all the space-station machinery was up and running, we were ready to work.

Our main job on Skylab was to perform scientific experiments. And there were lots of them to do. Two of our most important tasks were to gather information about the Earth and the Sun. Owen Garriott, a physicist, concentrated his work on the Sun, using a special telescope and other equipment. You probably know that the Sun, our nearest star, is a super-hot

The Skylab III astronauts. Owen, Jack, and I are about to enter the van that would take us to the launch pad. [NASA]

ball of gas more than 93 million miles from the Earth. But you may not know that sometimes the outer part of the Sun erupts, shooting hot material far out into space. We took pictures of several of those eruptions and of many other fascinating solar events. In fact, when the mission was over, we had taken more than 75,000 photos of the Sun!

Owen also took charge of some special passengers on board the spacecraft—two spiders named Arabella and Anita. But the spiders weren't stowaways. They were part of a science experiment that was thought up by a schoolgirl named Judith Miles. Judith—and scientists back on Earth—wanted to see if spiders could build their webs in the weightlessness of space. At first, Arabella seemed a little confused and couldn't spin a very good web. But soon she made a perfect one. She and Anita both became very successful "spider-nauts."

Jack Lousma spent a lot of his time taking photographs of Earth. As Skylab commander, I did experiments, too, and kept all the scientific work running smoothly. And do you want to know something? Jack, Owen, and I turned out to be a great Skylab team.

Once we settled into our life in space, we were able to put in many long, productive days. It was fun to cooperate, with each man doing his best. Some of our work was especially rewarding, because it directly helped everyday people back on Earth. For example, we used Skylab's Earth scanners to report on weather patterns and track huge ocean storms that threatened towns and cities. We also used the scanners to help researchers find water under a desert in Africa. I had many proud moments as an astronaut, and very near the top is the work Owen, Jack, and I did on Skylab III.

Another important task on Skylab was to learn about how our bodies adapted to life in space. Space is very different from the Earth. There is no pull of gravity to make things "heavy" so they will stay put in one place. Instead, anything that is not fastened down— including people—just floats. Like some other astronauts, my crew and I all felt "space sick" for our first few days in orbit. Mostly, we felt nauseous when we moved around. If we held still, we were soon okay again—but then we couldn't get any work done. We tried to strike a balance between moving around to work and feeling sick, and after three or four days things went better. We gradually got used to weightlessness. Then, zero-G (G is for gravity) was fantastic.

Like magic, I could do things that would be impossible on Earth. If I wanted to go from one place in the space station to another, all I had to do was give myself a little push in the right direction. Away I zoomed, like a floating Superman! For fun I tried some gymnastics—fancy twists and graceful somersaults. It was great. If only I could have had those super moves when I was a gymnast in college!

Just as on my Moon trip, the only time I didn't enjoy floating was when it was time to sleep. Then, I would have to strap myself down tightly in my bunk. I liked the feeling of being snug in bed.

Reading data in the ward room of the Skylab space station. [NASA]

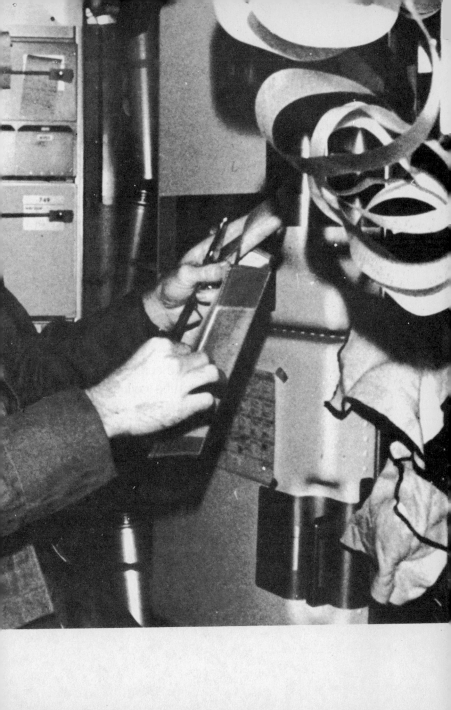

You may be wondering how astronauts do other things in space—such as eating and drinking and going to the bathroom. Food and drinks come in containers, like plastic cartons and pouches. These keep food from floating away while we're eating it. Can you imagine trying to eat beef stew while it floats around your kitchen? We usually used forks or spoons (or fingers) to eat with, and a lot of our food was in a thick sauce or gravy. That was so it would stick to the utensil and not float away before it reached a hungry mouth! We squirted our drinks, such as orange or grapefruit juice, into our mouths from plastic cartons.

Going to the bathroom in weightlessness is also more complicated than on Earth. To keep body wastes from floating around in Skylab, there was an air-suction system that pulled them into waste containers. A little cup attached to an air-suction tube collected urine. Wastes in the toilet were collected in plastic bags in the same way. We put the plastic bags into a special oven that dried the solid waste. Then each bag was stored to be brought back to Earth.

Every few days, we performed medical tests to see how our bodies were functioning. Why? Because without proper exercise, the body can react in harmful ways to weightlessness. For instance, in zero-G, bones and heart muscles can grow weaker, because they don't have to work hard. On Earth, that work is part of what keeps bones and muscles strong. So, to stay healthy, every day we scheduled one hour of exercise. Usually I rode the exercise bicycle, and sometimes just for fun I went tumbling in circles around Skylab's water tanks.

Living and working in Skylab, we had plenty of chances to look down at many different parts of our planet. Skylab circled the Earth about once every ninety minutes. That added up to about fifteen times every day. During our fifty-nine-day trip, we traveled more than 21 million miles, going around and around the Earth. On each orbit, we passed over one half of the Earth in daytime and over the other half in night. And over and over again, I got a special, colorful treat—seeing the lovely red, orange, and blue of a sunrise or a sunset.

At night, we sometimes saw a bright glow of light from a big city like New York or Chicago, while everything else was mostly black. In daytime, there was much more to observe, especially if we looked carefully. For example, did you know that the Pacific Ocean is a lighter color of blue than the Atlantic Ocean? That's how it looks from space. And I was amazed at the size of the Soviet Union and Asia— even from fast-moving Skylab, they seemed to go on and on forever. If the famous general Napoleon could have seen the Soviet Union from space, I don't think he would ever have tried to invade it! I also loved seeing snow-ringed volcanoes in New Zealand and the sharp, icy peaks of the Himalayas.

Near the end of our mission, I got a fantastic look at the Earth—and a whole lot of space—from outside Skylab. Owen Garriott and I "walked" in space, changing film in some cameras (more pictures!) and making repairs on other instruments on the outside of the space station. It was the hardest day I worked during the Skylab mission but also the most fun.

After eight busy and fruitful weeks in Skylab, my crew and I prepared to return to Earth. We cleaned up and packed away the equipment that the next crew would need when they arrived. We also stuffed three flight suits so that it looked as if astronauts were already in them. Then we left them sitting in the crew quarters like ghosts. We carefully kept the three phantom spacemen a secret. When the next crew arrived, they were shocked to find a welcoming party!

Then we moved back into the spacecraft that had brought us to Skylab and undocked. Slowly, rocket thrusters pushed us away from the space station. In a way, it was a sad good-bye, because we had done so much good work in our workshop in space. A few hours later we splashed down in the blue Pacific Ocean, off the coast of California.

Skylab was my last mission into the wonderful world of space. But it wasn't the end of my days as an as-

Owen working outside Skylab on an experiment whose purpose was to collect interplanetary dust particles.
[NASA]

tronaut. When I returned to Earth, I began work as commander of the backup crew on a project called Apollo-Soyuz. It was a team effort of the United States and the Soviet Union. For the first time, American astronauts and Soviet cosmonauts would meet in space and work together in a space station.

The training was very interesting. The best part was working with Soviet cosmonauts. We trained with them three times in the United States and three times at Star City, just outside Moscow. There are many differences between our space program and theirs, but there are also a lot of similarities between Soviet and American people. I'm looking forward to the United States and the Soviet Union flying many joint space missions in the future. Would you like to go along on a trip like that?

The next few years of my life were full of changes and challenges. After Apollo-Soyuz I worked on an exciting new project, the space shuttle program. I also retired from the Navy. It hardly seemed that more than twenty years full of hard work and fun had gone by since I'd first become a Navy pilot. Another change was difficult: Sue and I divorced. But at NASA I was named acting chief astronaut. That meant that I would be in charge of training new astronauts, including the first American women to fly into space.

And something else was happening in my life, too. As a pilot and astronaut, I'd had so many dreams come

Here I am leaning on my trusty T-38 jet. As an astronaut, I flew this high performance airplane around the country on NASA business.

true. Now, day by day, a new dream was starting to grow.

I was no longer training for a space flight. Clay and Amy were growing up and going off to college. All of a sudden, there was spare time for something else I loved to do: painting. Ever since my first art class while I was a test pilot at Pax River, I had studied painting. Most of my pictures were of flowers and seashores. And after all those years of practice, they were starting to be professional-looking.

Then, one day, a friend made a startling suggestion: She said I should stop painting flowers and seashores. Instead, she said, why not paint the Moon?

At first, I didn't know what to think. Paint the Moon? But the idea didn't go away. Pretty soon, it was all I could think about. I'd had so many wonderful times as an astronaut on Apollo 12. I had been lucky enough to see the beautiful blue ball of Earth and to walk on the rocky hills of the Moon. Painting what I had seen would let me share those adventures with others. One of them would be a fine lady named Leslie, who became my second wife.

Trying to do something new and difficult is always a little bit scary. Could I really paint the story of Apollo? I wanted to, very much. And, once more, I was willing to work long and hard.

Not long afterward I took a deep breath and made my decision. From then on, I was a painter. But my astronaut years would not be forgotten. They would be my inspiration. And even after I resigned from the corps of astronauts, I knew that part of me would always be a sailor to the stars.

CHAPTER 8

I have to say it one more time: I have been so lucky in my life. I have always had a dream to hold onto and to work for. Most mornings nowadays I am busy doing my painting by 8:00 A.M. I use "space age" paints called acrylics. They have plastic in them, which helps the paint last a long time. And instead of painting on old-fashioned canvas, I brush the acrylic paint on hard Masonite board. The hours go by fast, because I am working hard following this new dream of mine. After all, with colors and brush strokes, I'm preserving the wonderful stories and adventures of Apollo.

All of my paintings have names, and each of them tells a story. It is hard to pick a favorite. But one that many people like is called "Too Beautiful to Have Happened by Accident." It shows Apollo 17 astronaut Gene Cernan on the Moon, with the lovely blue and white ball of Earth in the black of space behind him. One of his hands, in a bulky space glove, is gently touching the American flag.

97

Too Beautiful to Have Happened by Accident. *Painting © 1983 Alan Bean.*

Helping Hands. *Painting © 1985 Alan Bean.*

I painted "Helping Hands" to show Pete Conrad and me working as a team on the Moon, taking a tool apart. Another painting tells a story I like very much. When I began the painting, it showed Gene Cernan and Jack Schmitt working near a Moon boulder. One day, when the painting was nearly done, Gene came over to my house to look at it. He said, yes, it showed things just as they had been that exciting day on the Moon. Apollo 17 was America's last Moon venture, and as usual the astronauts had been extremely busy. In fact, Gene said just a little bit wistfully, there was one thing he wished he had done on the Moon but hadn't thought of in the rush. He wished he had written the name of his daughter, Tracy, in the moon dust on a boulder.

Left: HOPES AND DREAMS, initial lay-in. *I wanted to create a painting to celebrate the flight of the space shuttle Discovery scheduled for the fall of 1988. This flight will signal the return of the space shuttle to flight status. No American has flown in space since the explosion of the space shuttle Challenger in January of 1986. I wanted the painting to be dramatic, and so I painted the most spectacular moment in all of space flight.*

Right: First major adjustment. *As I studied the painting, I kept asking myself, "How can I show that this will carry with it the hopes and dreams of so many people?" I thought of a sunrise, symbolic of the dawning of a new day. But the bright sun and the flame from the rockets looked much the same. Perhaps the shuttle passing just in front of a rainbow would work.*

 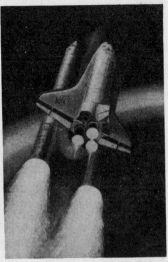

Left: Second major adjustment. *The painting was beginning to feel better. To me, the rainbow was symbolic of hope, but the shuttle looked too large in relation to the rainbow. I carefully repainted the shuttle to make it a little smaller. But it still didn't feel completed.*

Right: Final adjustment. *Over the course of the next week, I studied the almost finished painting. What did it still need? Then I remembered my first lay-in and how dramatic the white shuttle seemed when it was set against the dark sky. I had lost some of that drama. If I moved the rainbow further away, then I could have the dark sky* and *the rainbow. I quickly repainted the rainbow. Finally, the painting was finished: it looked right and it felt right. It reminded me of what Frederick "Rick" Hauck, the commander of Discovery, had once said to me: "The hopes and dreams of the American people for the future of the United States Manned Space Program will be riding with us when we lift off."* Hopes and Dreams—*no other title would do.*

I thought to myself: That's just like a loving father. And the story gave me an idea. I could not send Gene Cernan back to the Moon to etch Tracy's name in moon dust. But with a few quick brushstrokes, I could do almost as well. A short while later the painting was finished. And anyone who looks closely at it can see, written on the side of a gray moon boulder, the letters T-R-A-C-Y. I retitled the painting "Tracy's Boulder."

To me, all of my paintings hold wonderful memories. I hope that others will like them, too. Apollo was a very special time in human history—it was the first time human beings visited a world other than our Earth. As astronaut Neil Armstrong said, exploring the Moon was a "giant leap" for mankind.

But the adventures of men and women in space are not over. In the future—*your* future—I believe astronauts will explore many new worlds in space. And maybe *you* will be one of those explorers.

What does it take to become an astronaut? Well, there are several basic requirements. In the future, just as now, young people who want to be astronauts will have to be physically fit. Almost certainly, they will have to have a college degree, too. So if you are thinking of an astronaut career, keep yourself strong in mind and body. When I was starting out, all astronauts were men, and most of them were former military test pilots. Today, the situation is different. Men and women from many walks of life may qualify. There are still pilots, but there are also lots of scientists, from fields including biology, oceanography, physics, and astronomy. I'm sure you have heard of Sally Ride, a physicist who was the first American woman in space.

In the years ahead, when people are living and working in space situations, we will need astronauts with many kinds of training. Some will be doctors and nurses, others will be space-station mechanics and plumbers. There will be a need for space construction workers to build and repair things, people to run computers, and one day, there may even be astronaut artists and journalists.

Some of these astronaut jobs probably lie far in the future—they will be things that *your* children might do. So what would I do today if I wanted to be an astronaut? What kinds of jobs would I be trying to prepare myself for?

If I were your age I would first try to find more information. I would start by writing to NASA in Washington, D.C., and ask how to become an astronaut. I would also read newspapers and magazines and watch for articles on the space program—now and in the future. There, I might get ideas for skills that tomorrow's astronauts will need. For example, astronauts of the future may be studying the Sun from space and learning how food plants grow in weightlessness. There will surely be other jobs I haven't even thought of. When I got information back, I would try to decide what subjects I could study in college to prepare myself. I'd keep in mind that many different kinds of training will be useful in space.

I would also start preparing myself. And I would plan ahead. First it is necessary to have a dream. If I already have one, that's wonderful. But if I don't, I would spend a lot of time thinking about what I'm good at and what I'm not so good at, what I like and what I don't like. We have the best chance of fulfilling our dreams if we pick something we're good at. But thinking and dreaming is only one half of the process. I would try to remember that action and work make dreams come true. If I found out that NASA will need geologist-astronauts, and I thought I might like geology, I would go to a library and start reading about that subject this week. If I liked it, I would keep on. If not, I would try learning about one of the other astronaut jobs. Whenever young people tell me they would like to become astronauts—or anything else— I always say that's great. And I always ask: What are you *doing* about it?

As I look back on my life and all of the things I was able to do, I sometimes remember that young boy from dusty little Wheeler, Texas. When I started out, I knew I loved airplanes. But before becoming a naval aviator, I had to learn that doing well in school was important. Also, I had to be willing to make the effort to study. As I naval aviator, I had to learn to plan and work to make my specific dreams come true by using principles explained in self-help books. As a test pilot, I had to learn to do my best, even on jobs that I didn't always like. To become an astronaut I had to keep trying even when things didn't go my way. And always I had to learn to keep a positive attitude even though often I failed on the road to success.

And one more thing. If you plan and work hard, expect to have some good things "just happen" to you. I have always had that kind of luck. I bet you'll have luck, too.

It is time now to end this book. I have enjoyed telling my story, and I hope you have enjoyed learning about the life of an astronaut. It has been a wonderful one for me. I'm proud of the work I did in space, and grateful that I had the chance to do it. And I know that more good work—and wonderful adventures—lie in store for the young space travelers of tomorrow. If that is your dream, I hope one of those travelers will be you.

About the Authors

Alan Bean was born in the town of Wheeler, Texas on March 15, 1932 and spent most of his childhood in the city of Fort Worth. Upon graduating from the University of Texas in 1955, he trained as a naval pilot and was assigned to Attack Squadron 44. When his five-year tour was over, he became a test pilot, and in 1963 he was selected as one of fourteen new astronauts for the Apollo missions, part of NASA's growing space program. In 1969, after intensive training, Alan Bean was asked to pilot the Lunar Module of Apollo 12, the United State's second lunar landing mission. He became the fourth person to walk on the Moon. Four years later he commanded the fifty-nine day Skylab III mission, the longest manned journey into space at that time. Alan Bean is also an artist. Since retiring from the Navy, he has devoted his time to painting scenes from the American experience in space.

Beverly Fraknoi is a science writer and editor who enjoys writing for young people. She lives with her family near San Francisco and has just completed her first novel for children.

Standing in front of the five engines of the Saturn V rocket. A rocket just like this started us on our journey to the Moon.